The TEST

written and illustrated by **Jenn Gregory**

credo
house publishers

Keep Shining Kozminskis

Jenn Gregory

The Test
Text copyright © 2020 by Jenn Gregory
Illustration copyright © 2020 by Jenn Gregory
All rights reserved.

Published in the United States of America by Credo House Publishers
a division of Credo Communications, LLC, Grand Rapids, MI
credohousepublishers.com

ISBN: 978-1-62586-174-0

Illustrations by Jenn Gregory
Interior design and typesetting by Sharon VanLoozenoord
Editing by Donna Huisjen

Printed in the United States of America
First edition

To all students,
but most especially the Class of 2020

One night Little Star said to Moon, shining bright,
"I've noticed a thing that does not seem quite right.

"It's only the ones who are under age three
Who find me a wonder and gaze dreamily."

"Kids no longer wish
    upon stars for pets
Or unicorns, love, peace,
    or lucky-duck bets.

"What's happened to stifle
    the people down there
Who once were so willing
    to dare and to care?"

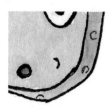

The wise Moon smiled softly and heaved a long sigh
Before she began to explain the sad why:

"One day recently was not like all the rest
For evil invaded the Earth with a test.

"A test not of reading or numbers or skill
But of people's wisdom, their faith, and their will.

"The people responded with courage, not fear—
New babies, a beacon of hope that sad year.

"Not all life is spoiled. Small kids still play with ease
And dream of becoming whatever they please:

"A fireman, a dancer, a pilot, a knight—
They dream and imagine, a future in sight.

"But dreams can get blurry,
   hope's gates can slam closed,
As children grow older
   and evil's exposed.

"It's easy to think all is well
   and ignore
Life's tragic disasters,
   the ozone that's torn,

"It's easy to sleep right through
   sadness and war,
Through drought, pain, and hatred—
   we've done it before.

"But sometimes the evil
   is hard to ignore.
On this day the trouble drilled down
   to the core,

"Broke life as we know it—
   unexpected alarm—
This worldwide pandemic would do
   untold harm."

Little Star cried great tears;
    he could now understand
Why wishes on stars that had once
    seemed so grand

Were losing their luster, their hope,
    their allure.
The future imagined no longer
    seemed sure.

"Oh when, and by what, can this tragedy end,
And who can contribute to help the world mend?"

"Kids and young grownups have knowledge and skill—
The courage, inventiveness, vision, and will.

"Today's tests no longer are science or lit.
They are all about patience, wisdom, and grit."

Moon held up the test paper for Little Star
And said, "The right answers will take the Earth far."

"But how will they know that those answers are right?"
And that is when Moon smiled full, big, and bright.

"They're smart and creative—a pivotal force.
This young generation will soon change the course.

"These new adults help, doing their best,
And accepting their role as the world's privileged guests.

"Respect for all creatures—their anthem rings clear,
Proclaimed eagerly, year after year.

"These bright young adults obey one simple rule:
To love one another is *the* greatest tool.

"So dry up your tears, my friend, Little Star.
I'm seeing a happy conclusion, . . . not far.

"What started on 9/11 (two thousand one)
Began a 'new normal' there under the sun,

"Accepted today without question by all,
Preparing the young to accept their new call.

"Earth's kids and young people, bookended by pain,
Will rise to the challenge without placing blame.

"The young, we all know, cannot do this alone.
The love from *all* people must first set the tone."

"Will they pass that new test, Moon—one hundred percent?"
"They will if their effort and time are well spent.

"They're in this together,
       so think about this—
On one thing particular
       they MUST insist:

"'Look UP every night
    to those lights far above
And keep wishing wishes
    and practicing love.'"

Little Star smiled brightly and said with great glee,
"I long for those kids to keep wishing on me!"

The wise Moon gazed down and caught sight of YOU.
May your dreams be fulfilled and your love remain true.

Made in the USA
Middletown, DE
18 October 2021